A CAREER WOMAN'S GUIDE TO SELF-LEADERSHIP

BY BIANCA ZENKEL

PASSIONPRENEUR® PUBLISHING

A CAREER WOMAN'S GUIDE TO SELF-LEADERSHIP

How to find the confidence and clarity to see your mountaintop and conquer it

BY BIANCA ZENKEL

PASSIONPRENEUR® PUBLISHING

Publishing information
Publishing and design facilitated by Passionpreneur Publishing
A division of Passionpreneur Organization Pty Ltd
ABN: 48640637529

Melbourne, VIC | Australia
www.passionpreneurpublishing.com

To my mum and daughter,
the women who inspire me every day
to become a better person.

TABLE OF CONTENTS

INTRODUCTION

Everything starts with dreams and a confident you; the rest is just a follow-up.

How many times have you been at crossroads? How many times have you chosen the compromise and remained on the same path due to fear of change or getting out of your comfort zone?

As I have been there on many occasions, my book is a real-life, authentic guide that helps you overcome these obstacles and progress to what you wish to become. It teaches you that everything starts with a dream, a desire to change, and a vision of the person you want to be, and explains the steps you must take to turn this into reality.

It takes you through my career journey and, with every chapter, gives you the necessary tools to unlock the true potential that you possess. You are a free person and you should have the freedom to choose your own path, without constraints.

On many occasions, I have been asked how I knew what the right choice was, the right move. The truth is, I didn't know, and there have been moments when the weight of other people's expectations, or the expectations of society, created a sort of paralysis that left me unable to move forward. But eventually, I had to learn how to take a risk and make things happen. I wasn't always prepared to jump to my next opportunity but, once I landed one, I made sure I worked very hard to make it a success. And most often, this success was achieved by growing my confidence and keeping a positive attitude towards change.

There are a few important life lessons that I have learned in the last twenty years that have proven to be the foundation of my career journey, and I will be sharing them with you. Perhaps the most important one is keeping a growth mindset and continuing your development. I started my career on a cruise line where my only real skill was speaking two languages: English and German. I then moved to aviation as cabin crew where I learned about safety, security, first aid, and customer service. I even had to learn a bit about engineering. From there, I moved into marketing where I have been for over fifteen years, starting as a communication executive and moving up on the career ladder to leadership roles.

Marketing is a dynamic profession and, to keep up with the changes, every year I study something new. Last year, I took a management course focused on diversity and inclusion from Yale University and, as I write this book, I am conducting research for my MBA dissertation, 'The RISE of Women in Leadership.'

I had a dream and I worked hard to turn this dream into reality. I went through moments of fear, guilt, and frustration but I also experienced moments of fulfilment and the satisfaction of achievement. When I felt stuck without a clear vision of how to escape the situation, I found a way to take things forward: I discovered the necessity of looking at things from a different perspective.

This book is about me and my career journey. My learnings, my failures, my successes, and the ingredients to make things happen.

It is the story of an ordinary girl who had a dream and simply followed it. I don't pretend to be a life coach or a psychologist or offer a recipe that will change your life forever. I found the confidence to open my heart in the hope that it will help you become the person you aspire to be.

Enjoy the read! I hope you find in these pages inspiration and practical tips to take the next steps in your own journey. It's an honour to walk it with you.

Bianca Zenkel

CHAPTER 1

FROM ROMANIA TO DUBAI

I have always believed that life demands that you move forward—and that you keep moving toward higher goals. From a very young age, the idea of participating in things that make an impact not only on me but on the people around me was something I found exciting. This excitement, this feeling of fulfilment, has offered me the motivation to keep moving forward.

I was born and raised in a little town in Romania where life seemed simple and people had well-established paths. There was a pre-written path for everyone, with very few examples of anyone moving away from that path. It was a very happy place where everyone knew everyone and there was an unspoken awareness of social rank—if you belonged to a particular family, you had to follow a predesignated career journey.

Until university, I consciously followed that path although, in some moments, things didn't go exactly right. But, once I finished university and realised that the offers in front of me were not fulfilling, I decided to break with the stereotypes and create my own journey.

My education has not been in Ivy League universities—not even close. I haven't practised the majors I studied. At university, my chosen majors of German and English didn't lead me toward a teaching career but instead somehow jump-started what was becoming my departure from small-town life and steps toward the big world.

YOU HAVE THE POWER TO CHANGE DREAMS INTO REALITY

This book is about the career journey of a small-town girl who took life into her own hands and travelled across continents in search of a place where she belonged, a place where she could find the opportunities she was looking for. I couldn't settle for what was in front of me just because it was an easier approach. That wasn't enough, it wasn't what I dreamed of. Sometimes, I had to pick up the broken pieces, start over, and keep going until it felt right. Some would say, 'It is too much! You need to stop and enjoy what you have created!' But I always wanted to be ready for the next step. My career to date is the result of continuous hard work and development. That's my recipe for success—that and the secrets to confidence and self-leadership that I have learned along the way. Across all these years, following this recipe was the only way I could progress and persevere.

Today, as I write this book, I have come very far from where I started and my motivation for writing the book came from the enormous number of people asking me, 'How have you succeeded?' and, 'What is the recipe behind it all?' And in many cases, there has been the sense that they think, *There must be somebody who has helped her. There must be a hidden way she has taken to reach this far.*

Sadly, or luckily, there isn't a magical way of making things happen. Across my entire journey, from the moment I graduated from school until now, it has been just me, and my story is based on the choices I made, the people I allowed to be part of my story, and my continuous drive to keep going.

Our career choices are a puzzle of pieces coming together.

I have always kept believing in myself and have focused on my strengths and skills to move forward. It hasn't always been easy. In my early years, I bravely decided to join a cruise ship for eight months and this marked the beginning of a very unexpected journey. There were feelings of fear—fear of rejection, embarrassment, and failure—as I was starting something I thought I was not prepared for. But it went well and that was the first moment I realised that we set our own limits and, as humans, we are so afraid of failure that we can boycott our own success.

Navigating the world on a cruise ship was a wonderful experience. It was my first exposure to different countries and cultures. But it wasn't something I would have wanted to continue. After eight months on the water, I decided to take to the skies and, with the benefit of the cruise experience, I secured a cabin crew contract with one of the world's biggest airlines, based in the United Arab Emirates, the place that has become my home for over sixteen years. From that point on, United Arab Emirates became a place of enormous opportunity and my career has been a journey of ups and downs that has evolved due to my desire to always rise higher than my expectations.

But these are jobs, right? Is this just a book about career? No, it isn't. Because, for me, my career was my path to finding confidence and meaning. It was my path to finding who I really am and want to be. We women find this sense of self in many ways. We also lose it in many ways, as we give our all to serve and nurture the people we love. So, I am writing about my journey of self-leadership, which I describe throughout this book as a hiking track that leads to the top of the proverbial mountain. This book guides you, my dear readers, through the preparation I had to do to set out on the track, and the many milestones and crossroads I passed to finally reach the top of my imaginary mountain.

NOTHING IS MAGIC, YOU ARE CREATING YOUR DESTINY

The decision to start this journey came from a place of frustration, pain, and limitation—a place that has nothing to offer and accepting it requires you to sacrifice your right to follow your dreams and be happy. My decision was to overcome all the limitations, ignore the status quo, destroy any expectations, and just follow my dreams. I grew up in an environment where risk-taking was encouraged and my family has always surrounded me with inspiration and motivation.

The preparation stage was very important for me and it took a few years of continuous hard work as, while I had the drive to keep going, I was missing much of the skill and knowledge I needed. You see, while this is your own track, there are many other people positioned at every step. To move higher, you need to keep a competitive edge. It's not a competition—as I said, this is your journey—but the people around you are going to be part of your journey and can be seen either as drivers to keep you moving forward or as obstacles.

Once I started my hike, I learned that one thing I need to grow stronger and always keep progressing is confidence. There have been many instances where my lack of confidence has hindered my ability to move forward and left me feeling uncertain and mired in fear, doubt, and confusion.

Building confidence is not something that happens overnight. It takes experience, failure, and hard work. Building up your skills and working on the person you wish to become is what makes you confident. The times you have failed and pulled yourself up, the times when you have transformed darkness into light, give you the strength and power to be confident. While I have made huge progress, I still have moments when doubt and fear invade my universe. The difference is that now I have the tools to move away from such feelings and bring back the confident me.

MAKING CHOICES ABOUT PEOPLE YOU ACCEPT TO BE PART OF YOUR LIFE

A very significant part of building my confidence was the extraordinary group of people that have been my support along this journey. This is a very important lesson I want you to always remember—without a network of people around you, it will be very difficult to succeed. You need people to motivate and inspire you, and to be there for you in moments of doubt and confusion.

Choosing the people who are going to make a difference in your career is almost an art. Along the way, you will learn to recognise people who are there to support and complement you, and those who are toxic. My twelve-year-old daughter once came home from school super disappointed that the girl she believed was her BFF had somehow let her down. For a twelve-year-old, everything can be dramatic, but it was hard to explain to her that sometimes the people you trust and love can disappoint and hurt you. Sadly, I am sure this will not be her last such experience.

People come and go in our lives, and our role is to filter and decide who we want to keep around, and who will add value and support our journey.

Throughout my career, I have met some amazing mentors and colleagues who have a very special place in my heart and I will always carry a piece of them in my work ethic and leadership journey. They have helped me model myself into the person I am today. These people are not just there to cheer you up but also to point out mistakes, identify areas of development, and challenge you. I have also met people who have pulled me down using manipulation and fake support while using me to fulfil their own goals. It takes time to learn how to fight and distance yourself from such individuals. My book will guide you through a subconscious system that will help you to find your real supporters with every step you take on your hiking track.

Another very important skill that will keep you on your hiking track is identifying your *purpose*. I know this can sound cliché and you may have been asked many times about your purpose without finding an answer. Just like you, I thought of purpose as something visionary that has nothing to do with real life and I was never able to articulate my purpose on the spot. But, somehow, the idea of doing things for a higher, more spiritual reason was something that I loved to believe in. Without always being consciously aware of it, I've always known that every action is geared toward making a change. The change related to creating something bigger and better and it was fuelled by the enthusiasm and effort I put into making things happen. Later, after I became a mother of two beautiful children and had a few more years of experience at work, I discovered that I am passionate about making a difference in women's lives.

WHAT IS MOST IMPORTANT TO YOU?

If you reflect on your own life or career story to date, what is most important to you? Where does your mind wander first thing in the morning when you wake up and just before you go to sleep? Creating a clear awareness of this will help you find the higher objective that will drive you to make things happen and bring you back to your initial track. You see, if you think of the hiking track, there is almost always a mountaintop, a map, a guide, and people who will make the journey with you. What is the meaning of that mountaintop? Why have you dedicated so much of your time and effort to the climb?

I was blessed with the support of many outstanding women who were on a mission to support other women. And I am not referring to any sort of tangible, material support. It was moral, inspirational, and motivational support. Their own life stories, struggles and successes, became the highest driver for me to continue my journey. And my biggest mentor was my mum. There isn't any situation where I won't think of what my mum would have done. I have always been amazed by her spirited energy and how she is always moving forward. She always had a group of women around her to either be inspired by or to inspire and her positive energy attracted people. In her career, she has seen generations of women grow and mature and she was there to guide and coach them. Even now, in her late sixties, she receives calls from ex-colleagues asking for advice. She has created a legacy and in her own world she is a role model that women are inspired to follow.

In moments of confusion or when at a crossroads, I hear the call of my little town—a call to return home where I will find solutions for any problem I may have. This is due to the confidence and sense of safety that my home and my mum inspire.

Another source of inspiration is looking at women who have made it and learning from their stories. How have they reached where they are now? What path have they taken? And across everyone, I find a common denominator: self-leadership. A skill that not only drives you through continuous achievement but also offers the opportunity to truly understand and connect with yourself. I will talk about self-leadership by providing real-life examples and explain how practising self-leadership has kept me going.

THE STORY BEGINS HERE

This book is a guide that takes you step by step through a series of episodes in my life that shows how a woman coming from a remote place in the world has made it to leadership positions in the corporate world. It will give you insights into my success but also into darker moments and the drivers that supported me across this journey to pull myself up and keep going. My aim is to inspire and motivate you to find the confidence to start out on your own hiking track and reach the imaginary mountaintop. There will be many obstacles on the way but, if you have the right tools, you'll know how to navigate your way there.

Finding and recognising the right tools for you is a never-ending process. The tools you need will change over time and need to be adjusted based on the height of your mountaintop and the obstacles you must overcome along your journey.

Reaching the top of your mountain is an unbelievable and highly emotional experience that will wipe out most of the dark moments and make you stronger and ready for the next adventure in your life. But once you reach one mountaintop, you are ready to conquer the world. You have done the work and have taken your life and career into your own hands. The rest will become part of your story.

The fact that you have chosen to read this book tells me that you are either thinking of making a change or are already close to setting out on your hiking track. Congratulations! You have made the first step, and I am proud of you. Now, read on and dream of your imaginary mountaintop and your own hiking track. This is your time to make a change and become the person of your dreams, to build the career you have always wanted.

There are many inspirational stories that you can relate to. Many outstanding people have started from very little and reached the absolute heights of success. But this is your story. Now, I want you to start working with me to put the puzzle of your dreams together. Before going on to the next chapter, take a moment to write down ten things that you dream about today but refuse to acknowledge could be transformed into reality due to different obstacles. Write them down for now and then continue to read.

Your 10 goals / dreams

_____

_____

_____

_____

_____

_____

_____

_____

_____

CHAPTER 2

STEP UP TO SELF-LEADERSHIP

Finding the confidence
to steer your own destiny

'You either walk inside your story and own it or you stand outside your story and hustle for your worthiness.'

— BRENE BROWN

The current landscape calls for women to take charge of their own careers. While I write this book, I am also working on my MBA dissertation titled 'The RISE of Women in Leadership,' and research has shown that, on a global scale, women increasingly tend to deny their personal needs and focus on the personal needs of their family and friends.

We are also sometimes impacted by our own desire to choose the easiest or most comfortable solutions when faced with adversity, options, or even our own dreams and aspirations. The truth is that while doing this might keep us in our comfort zone, the results will be insignificant.

If you are a woman who aspires to make career or life changes, by the end of this chapter you will be ready to start your journey towards change. Think of this book as your personal invitation to a hiking journey up your imaginary mountain.

THE FREEDOM OF DREAMING

As children, we often hear that everything is possible and you can be whatever you want to be. It's okay to dream of being Superman or a Policewoman who fights crime or a Doctor or a Teacher. But as we grow, our wings are broken and that universe of childhood filled with light, hope, and colour transforms into an obstacle course.

When I was about ten years old, I started to enjoy acting, drama, and stage exposure. I loved the attention of the audience and would audition to get the main character's role. It was something that captivated me and my parents and school were supportive. Fast forward to the time I went for a walk with my dad and we were discussing college applications. I told my dad I would like to pursue an acting career and he started laughing and said that he would pass. It wasn't a complete shock as I was expecting some sort of constructive feedback but the idea that the universe once open to me was not there anymore was jarring.

Most of our dreams and aspirations are driven by tangible aims and tactical thinking, by what we find to work in the moment, and by what we and society believe we deserve as our status. We internalise such standards and use them as a benchmark in our life because they have been the backbone of our world.

We always go back to the happy moments of our childhood, which I believe represent the foundations of our dreams and hopes. The image of that kid who was free and full of creativity is something that we continue to cherish.

My little childhood universe was very limited and confined to my own country but I remember many nights sitting outside with my mother, looking up to the sky and thinking of what the universe might hold and internally creating my exploration journey. Right then, in that moment, without knowing it, I created my own hiking track. The feeling of joy, excitement, and enthusiasm, and the fact that my mother was next to me, giving me the psychological safety that allowed me to have big dreams and hopes, is something that I go back to every time I need a push to get back on the right track.

THE JOURNEY TO DISCOVERY

After college graduation, I tried for a few months to understand what my universe looked like and what opportunities I had as a fresh graduate. Traditional ideas were put in front of me, things that my family and friends had all done. For me, that was not enough. The image of stars was coming back and I knew there was much more that I could do, much more to discover.

This was one of the most challenging times of my life, as I was trying to escape the many career openings that I had access to. It was hard as I was trying to resist the urge to just accept my fate and choose to be happy no matter what. Like many of you, I tried multiple companies, functions, and interviews, but nothing was working.

The event that finally made me determined to escape this agony was my first and last attempt to become a journalist. In my search for answers, I read every newspaper and magazine that was published and, in a regional newsletter, I found an ad placed by the newspaper itself and looking for aspiring journalists. I applied and was immediately called for an interview. It was a very exciting time and the entire world looked different that morning as I travelled to the newspaper's offices for my interview.

When I arrived, I felt my enthusiasm melt away. There was a large room filled with a strong smell of cigarettes and at least a hundred candidates. I wanted to keep an open mind and think of this experience as the beginning of a wonderful career. It was hard holding on in that moment as our task was to go to the train station, write an article, and submit it to the publication. It was a forty-minute walk to the train station and when I arrived it was empty. No trains, no travellers—it was deserted.

The noticeboard showed the station expected one train a day and that was all I could see around me. This snippet of information guided me to put a positive spin on things and write an article about possible investments to attract travellers and transform the station into a hub. Writing the article felt great. I submitted it a few hours later and was asked to wait for feedback. Two hours later, I was called in by the editor and was given the feedback that I was a very lovely girl but journalism was not for me.

THE PAIN OF LEARNING
TO DEAL WITH REJECTION

The shock was difficult to bear. My astonishment at the strength of his rejection left me unable to feel my legs or talk. I just stood there in front of this man, unable to decide what to do next. I'm not sure if this man who had posted the ad for an 'aspiring journalist' understood my condition, but he excused himself and wished me the best of luck. As I found the strength to walk out, there were only dark clouds ahead of me. This was the opportunity, this was the breakthrough I had been waiting for. This was the only chance I had to build my career. I felt guilt and anger as my entire universe was destroyed in a moment. I felt like I was in a trap. The universe was speaking to me and it seemed as though this was a sign that I should accept my fate and the future I was running away from.

That evening, my mom came to my room and showed me pictures of us looking up at the sky. I burst into tears as I felt that universe of freedom was just a dream, a fairy-tale story. My mom kissed my cheeks, took my hands in hers and asked me, 'Do you remember what your biggest wish was when you looked at the stars?'

'To discover the universe,' I answered.

'And why are you in search of that dream?' she continued.

This was the event that completely changed my life and brought me back to the right path.

A few days after that, supported by my parents, I took the decision to join a cruise ship. The company that was recruiting cruise ship staff agreed to put me on a waiting list as they needed German speakers and told me they would call me back in eight to twelve months. It wasn't exactly a confidence boost but, in that moment, I decided to make it happen. For eight weeks, I travelled between my town and the city where the recruiting agency was located. Leaving every morning at 5.30 am and returning home at 7 pm, I went to see in person if there was any update.

The travel was not easy—late December, very low temperatures, snow, and mostly in trains with broken windows and no heating. In early February, as I arrived and took my place in the waiting room, the phone rang and I overheard a conversation about a new ship that needed German-language staff. I jumped off my seat and told everyone that I was a German and English speaker and ready to embark on the ship. That day, I had six interviews with different people and was offered an eight-month contract as a tour operator.

FINDING THE CONFIDENCE TO STEER YOUR DESTINY

On the way home, I had a flashback of my journey to that point and realised how deep desires come to the surface when you need them to. I connected to myself and my inner voice and understood that it's not easy to take an unconventional path. It takes willpower and confidence to push forward and not give up. The realisation came with a sense of power and I knew I had to make things happen and remain devoted to my goal.

I consider this episode to be one of the learning curves that have defined my career path and journey. It was decisive in making me consider things from a different perspective and look beyond the ordinary. That girl who was told that journalism was not for her and to find a different career path is now writing a book.

The truth is that a career journey is something that each of us has, and it is driven by our choices, commitment, grit, and desire to make it happen. I have envisioned my career journey as a hiking track that will lead me to an ultimate goal, represented by the top of a mountain. This is a metaphor I have created to guide me with every step. This hiking track I am going to share with you will guide you while you build your career. You will be confronted with adversity, doubt, and trials, but there will also be opportunities and chances along the way.

The chapters of this book outline my own hiking track and I'll share with you my struggles and dark moments but also the most outstanding experiences. Overall, you will understand my motivation and my drive to keep going.

The main idea is that when you find yourself at a crossroads, as I have on several occasions, you will be faced with choices—choices that will guide you toward your imaginary mountain. With every chapter, you will reach a new milestone and I'll ask you to write down challenges, motivations, and developments so that by the end of the book you will have created your hiking track, your own story.

This is your time to rise and shine, to create your own destiny. A recent article in the *Harvard Business Review* reported that during the COVID-19 pandemic, '54 million women around the world left the workforce, almost ninety per cent of whom exited the labor force completely.'[1] This is not the place where we want to be. But, indeed, it is true that we are often the first to shut down our dreams to support family and friends. I do not write this to judge, but to acknowledge the reality we are going through and, sadly, when women leave the workforce, the losses are major. I am not claiming that staying in the game and facing adversity is easy, but I would proudly say that I am one of the people who refuse to give up and will keep trying until I get to the desired outcome. Once there, the feeling of fulfilment is phenomenal.

Our time is now. In this book, I will take you through five vital stops on your road to self-leadership success and the discovery of your own Everest mountain.

1. **Understand your base of transformation**
   You've *got the power* to change things. If you have decided that it is time to reconnect with that little girl you used to be, with dreams and goals, you need to look at the big girl you are now and understand what skills you need to build, what gaps you need to fill, and what trade-offs you need to make. Think about the preparation you need to be ready for a real Everest

---

[1] Link to article: https://hbr.org/2022/03/when-women-leaders-leave-the-losses-multiply I believe it will add credibility but not sure if it is a standard procedure. https://hbr.org/2022/03/when-women-leaders-leave-the-losses-multiply Hougaard, Carter, & Afton March 8, 2022

hike—you will never commit to such an action without a few months, or perhaps many years, of work.

First steps and new beginnings are energising and fun but also daunting. The decision to start something new is the most important step. The base of the mountain (first base) is where you find hope for new beginnings and people cheering you on for making this decision—a place of serenity where you look up and see your goal. You are unable to see the whole track but imagine it won't be easy. You visualise the satisfaction of being there and create a mental image that you want to keep in your mind and heart.

2. The confident you

The path or hiking track is in front of you and you embark on this great adventure. You build confidence as you progress and see the possibilities. You celebrate the first milestones of success. As the road gets steeper and more difficult, you try to overcome each obstacle, one thing at a time, one step at a time, trying to keep that vision you had at the beginning of the hike alive. You sense the atmosphere and environment becoming hostile. People who were cheering for you are not there anymore but you keep going. Thoughts of desperation and fear will invade your mind and soul and you'll want to give up. Dark feelings of going back to what you knew before will creep up on you more often. The harder the track gets, the harder you must fight these feelings. It will be an internal war that you must win.

Confidence is what will keep you moving forward. With every step, you will go higher and conquer your dark feelings and emotions. Your confidence will grow and take you to the next step. This hike is taking you to the place of your dreams and the decision to move forward belongs entirely to you. The choices you make now will impact the person you'll become tomorrow. And if you need encouragement, remember who you were before you started.

3. The personal leadership paradigm

You keep going because the vision you have represents the future, the creation of a new life, the scope for you and your daughters, for all women who are striving to reach the top but don't dare to start. Your aim is to make a change that has an impact and demonstrates that things in life are possible if you have grit, determination, and strength. My ultimate goal is to create a better world for my daughter, a world where gender inequity and social pressure are no longer part of the conversation. And you, the women on the hiking track, think of the impact you'll have on yourself and the world around you once you reach that mountaintop. Your path and goal are becoming part of your identity, providing your unique values.

You are living proof that everything is possible if you strive to make it happen. Our path is built from the decisions we make. It is created by how we navigate through challenges and opportunities. With every step you take, you are closer to the top of the mountain, and this entire journey will not only build your resilience and confidence but will give you the courage to control your own path.

This journey will become your self-leadership discovery. It will be about self-discipline, strong mental health, strategy, and using all the resources around you with intelligence. The process of making this journey will give you insight into what is needed to achieve goals. With this accumulated knowledge, you will be able to influence others to walk the path.

My career journey has been filled with wonderful people. People who I will be forever grateful to for trusting me when I was at my lowest, for encouraging me to keep going when I was only heating stones and moving with desperation from failure to failure. And, most of all, for believing in me. These people were there for me because they'd been on this path before. They recognised the spark and determination and they only gave me a hand when I asked for it.

4. Defining yourself

This is what I am doing now by sharing my story and hoping that it will resonate with you and influence you to direct your hike toward your dream.

Change can be scary but also exciting. Daring to escape your comfort zone is the first sign that you are willing to go the extra mile and make this happen. You won't reach the top of the mountain, your dream, if you are not prepared to take the hike with its beautiful sunsets and cold, snowy days. But once you are there and you've made it, the feeling is unbelievable on all levels. It will be healing for all your guilt, fear, and moments of failure, and you'll be grateful for life. You will ask, 'What's next?' And there will be another mountain and another. But you'll be ready to take a much higher hiking track. There will be obstacles and crossroads. You will have to make decisions that might be scary. You will cry and sob and want to go back to a safe space. You'll feel lonely and sometimes unable to breathe and you will question your integrity and confidence. All of these feelings and emotions are a normal response to moving toward something great that will lead you to be the person you want to be.

5. Women supporting women

One of the forces that helped me reach this point in my life is a great network of successful, inspiring, and beautiful women. Being part of this network, I found my strength and my voice and worked on my confidence. Every day, we see women sacrifice themselves for what they believe to be the greater good. In an article written in early 2022, Katie Bishop reported that due to unconscious biases in the workplace, women's greater responsibility for childcare, and outright discrimination, women still hold just 23% of executive positions and 29% of senior manager positions globally, despite making up 40% of the workforce.[2]

This won't change overnight and, while some organisations are taking major steps to close the gap, there are still many things that need to be done. We have a role to play here—we need to persist and make sure our voices are heard. It is our responsibility to support each other in dark times and cheer for each other in happy times. Many times while writing this book, I have told myself that my story is ordinary and does not have the commercial buzz or glam of a fairy-tale. But I kept going because I know my story is relatable and authentic and I have a message that will inspire others to keep going.

In the previous chapter, I asked you to write down ten dreams that life's other commitments often overshadow. Now,

---

2 https://www.bbc.com/worklife/article/20220603-why-women-have-to-sprint-into-leadership-positions.

I want you to look at your ten goals and write down why are they important to you.

Your 10 goals / dreams

_____

_____

_____

_____

_____

_____

_____

_____

_____

As you read the chapters to follow, everything will start to make sense. We are about to start our journey and I am hoping that by the end of it you will already be embarking on your hiking track.

CHAPTER 3

THE BASE OF YOUR TRANSFORMATION

When you connect the dots and are ready to
start the journey to becoming the NEW YOU

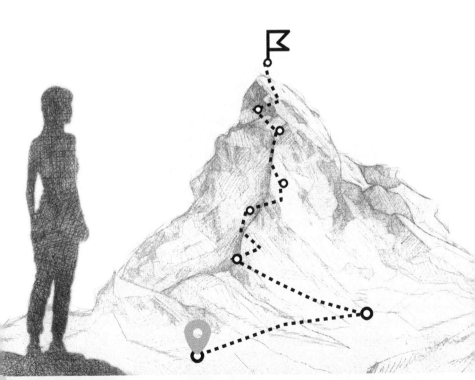

*'The moment you take responsibility for
everything in your life is the moment you can
change anything in your life.'*

— HAL ELROD

THE RIGHT TO DREAM AND ASPIRE

Many times, we dream, we make aspirational plans. We visualise parts of our life that are not right and that we would love to change. We feel this urge that drives us to hope and to see possibilities, alternatives, and a journey to make our dreams possible. The challenge is that on most occasions we kill this urge with our own fears. We decide to take the easier, more comfortable route and make peace with ourselves by trusting that it will work out.

I have walked this path many times. I've told myself that the effort of going the extra mile is not worth it. While it would feel comfortable for a while and I would be pleased with my decision, I would soon feel my life was lacking excitement and spark. I also went through moments of doubt and despair when I told myself it would get better without putting any effort or thought into how it would get better and what I needed to do to make things better.

By the end of this chapter, you will learn what the baseline is for your transformation. You will learn what inspires and motivates you. At the end of this journey, you will arrive at the baseline of your imaginary mountain and be ready to hike.

HAVING THE CONFIDENCE TO FIND YOUR OWN VOICE

How often have you killed your aspirations out of fear and lack of confidence?

Early in my career, I had the opportunity to meet two extraordinary women, Ashley and Wafa, who were images of perfection in my eyes. They were at the top of their careers, highly qualified executives with strong powers of decision-making. But at the same time they were humble, personable, and down to earth. They had it all and they made it look natural and easy. My observations from the outside were based on the immaculate way they presented themselves, the confident tone of their voices, and the way they approached complicated tasks calmly and with ease. Deep down in my heart, I wanted to have that corporate ease and spark. I remember watching them from the corner of my eye as they moved around the office and my desire to be part of their circle.

My choices were in front of me. At that time, I was tormented by how my heavy Romanian accent and lack of experience set me apart from my co-workers who were mostly native English speakers who had gone to college in the United States. I felt guilty and ashamed and my lack of confidence made me want to hide and blocked my creativity, preventing me from developing new ideas. I often felt the expectations placed on me were unfair and I misjudged people around me because I was unable to speak up and see that behind every experience, it was just me.

After a few weeks of struggle, I failed to execute a simple task. I was called into my manager's office and my feeling of guilt took over before the conversation even started. My hands were sweating, and tears rolled uncontrollably down my cheeks. I remember apologising, though my manager had said nothing. I didn't know exactly why I had been called into their office but as I agonised one of these two extraordinary women, Ashley, came in. When she saw me, she asked if I could walk with her.

We went into a meeting room and talked for hours. This was my first mentorship lesson with a person I admired. It was during these few hours that I realised I was in charge of my career. Yes, maybe the situation was not perfect, but it was up to me to change it. It was in that second that I had an enlightening moment and created my hiking track as I realised the possibilities were endless.

FINDING PEOPLE WHO WILL STAND BY YOUR SIDE TO GUIDE AND MOTIVATE

Thinking back, I believe the first lesson for me was the importance of having a person I admired and trusted on my side. As we start our careers, having a mentor is invaluable.

That day, she coached me to see how successful my journey had been up to that point and to move to the next point I needed to reach to grow and develop.

From that day for almost a year, I worked to understand my fears and what I could do to overcome them. I registered for an international marketing course at the Oxford College of Marketing and hired a language coach to improve my English in parallel with a Business English course. For six months, my life was divided between work and study. It was hard work that helped me regain confidence and add value to my career. It allowed me to reflect on my weaknesses and find the strength to accept them and find solutions.

It was a time when I better connected to myself and embarked on a journey of building confidence. It didn't come overnight, but with every step I took toward building a new skill, I did better at my job and improved my results. I also started to mingle with people from different nations and create a network of friends which later helped me to open up and be my own person.

During that time, I discovered that I had no lack of ideas or solutions to problems. I learned that I am highly creative and this often gave me the edge to meet a challenge. As my communication skills improved, I got involved in more projects and the tasks in front of me were more challenging.

PEOPLE ARE CONNECTED BY COMMON DREAMS AND DESIRES

One of the things that stood out for me was managing the end-to-end process of a media interview with the BBC which had accepted an invitation to write an article about the company I was working for. I remember running into Ashley's office that day and shouting, 'The BBC is coming.' She misheard my enthusiastic shout as, 'BABY C is coming,' so it was a very confusing moment. It was only when I repeated, 'The BBC is coming for the interview and reportage, and I am in charge,' that her face lit up, and she said simply, 'You've got this.'

And she was right. There were nerves, stress, and moments of despair, but it was very different than it had been in the past because my enthusiasm, passion, and confidence kicked in and overtook all other emotions. Once the interview process was over, I realised how much I loved being in the driver's seat, taking responsibility, and that feeling of achievement.

The success of this experience brought me the opportunity to work on the company's corporate newsletter. It was a new experience that required a different skill set and the idea of working on something new for which I was unprepared brought moments of doubt. The difference here was that I had people around me with whom I could talk and ask for help.

That day, I met Wafa for lunch. We spoke about the new challenge in front of me and I highlighted my doubts. Wafa is the type of person who exudes confidence on every occasion and transforms everything she touches into success. I've often asked what her secret is and she always laughs and says, 'There is no secret. It is just hard work and me.' One thing she told me during lunch was that the only person who can make the difference between a successful and unsuccessful project was me and my passion and desire to make things work.

At that point, I was not convinced and felt it was something of a cliché. But as I started working on the newsletter—dealing with strict deadlines, navigating different stakeholders, gaining approvals, and managing multiple people—I understood Wafa's words. There were many occasions when I reached a dead-end without visible solutions. There have been many occasions where I could have been happy with something mediocre, without trying to put in the effort to improve it. All these choices were mine. It was me who found the energy and commitment to move forward and get things done without settling for what was easier. There would be many sleepless nights and late meetings with editors but the newsletter was always out as promised.

UNDERSTANDING HOW TO LEARN FROM EVERY EXPERIENCE

As you build your confidence and grow, multiple avenues open in front of you and you need to keep going. You need to take advantage of every opportunity and learn from experience. While I was writing briefs for articles and interviewing colleagues, I had the opportunity to learn so much more about what private aviation stands for. I had the opportunity to speak to colleagues I would never have approached and began to create a name for myself. I learned from many mistakes, hours of reading and research, and had good advisors on my side. What Wafa said became one of my deepest learnings and I have been acting on the wisdom of her words for years.

We often find ourselves in judgemental environments but sometimes they are in our imagination. Due to a lack of confidence, we feel enormous social pressures that give us the feeling of not belonging. Sometimes, this feeling of social rejection drives us toward guilt and thoughts of not deserving to be there. It is a struggle. A continuous fight with our own sense of being able to power through and navigate such intense chemistries. The idea here is that you have the opportunity to choose the people you want to be with and, in most cases, these people are the ones who can offer proper psychological safety where you have the opportunity to grow and develop your skills without the pressure of always being under attack.

IT MIGHT START WITH A MOMENT OF DOUBT

My personal journey started in a moment of complete doubt and sadness, a moment that brought in despair and froze my heart and soul. But that moment was what I needed to make a change and understand that my negative emotions were not worth it. There was no going back and in that moment I decided to envision my own top of the mountain and my hiking journey.

The first question you must ask yourself is 'What are my deepest fears and what is the hidden black spot that is holding me back from being the person I want to be?' For me, it was the lack of confidence generated by the feeling that I was not meeting that perfect marketing vision of an excellent narrator with a melodic English accent. This fear was allayed in a conversation I later had with Ashley about my choices for finding a way to solve the problem. Ashley pointed out that I should shake up this tendency I had to look at people superficially and dig deeper. It took me time to understand the meaning of her words but later I understood that having a melodic accent does not take you far without also having a clear message, creative ideas, and passion.

The second question to ask yourself is, 'What type of professional do I want to become?' To answer this question, you must draw a line and write down where you are now and where you want to go. Envision your journey and think of what skills you want to gain in time.

Think of your hiking journey and the preparation you must do before you can reach the base of the mountain. You might already be at the base or you might be far from it. So, to start your hiking journey, you must prepare your psyche and your mental health, have financial support, and people who will cheer you on during this journey.

Your career journey is no different. Complete this exercise before you read on:

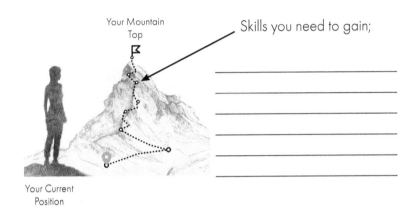

Your Mountain Top

Skills you need to gain;

_____

_____

_____

_____

_____

_____

Your Current Position

Due to Ashley and Wafa, I learned very early in my career the power of mentorship and having a guiding voice behind you. Our friendship continued long after the 'BABY C' episode and even today, though we are in different countries, we enjoy a strong connection and engagement. I've also learned that such people are hard to find and I was lucky to have such highly motivated mentors early in my career.

EVERYTHING STARTS WITH YOUR DESIRE TO CHANGE

It was phenomenal to hear how our stories related to each other. Both Ashley and Wafa started in junior roles and, through an immense commitment to achievement, they made it to the top of the career ladder. Wafa is an absolute gem and she has more than once reached the ultimate goal but then had to change and start from scratch due to external forces. Her desire to move forward and be successful has swiped away any obstacle or challenge she has faced during her time.

As you prepare to reach the base of your mountain or, if you are there already, it is important to surround yourself with people who have already reached their mountaintop or have reached the top of multiple mountains—people who have found the strength to keep going and are happy to cheer for you and be there when you need them. Each story is different and each mountain has a different story, but your attitude to making things happen is the common thread. It always starts with the desire to change and see things from a different perspective.

For this to work, you need to practise self-honestly and fully understand the person you are with all your strengths and weaknesses. It is important to have an image of the mountain you want to climb and the journey you must go through to reach that place. From my experience and that of most of my friends and mentors, I can say that there is no fast track. There is a journey of many feelings and events that will eventually lead you to where you want to go. The preparation is the first significant starting point. You may want to start a hike without proper gear or adequate physical training, and you could, but you won't make it very far.

You also need to surround yourself with people who will be there for you to support you but also bring you back to the right path when needed and help build your hiking tools and skills. Make a mental note of such people and make sure you create opportunities to engage with them. You will know they are right for you from the easy way you connect and have chemistry.

When your current circumstances do not serve you and feelings of fear, disappointment, guilt, and anger occupy your days and nights, it is time to change—change the course of your life. This is not something that happens overnight. It takes courage, determination, and patience. And it takes time.

You need the courage to tell yourself that you deserve a better life and a better outlook. The universe gives you opportunities. You just need to drive its energy towards you and make things happen. Once you make the decision to change, visualise the journey, the next step and the next—you won't be able to see the full journey but you will get closer to the final target with each step.

This is the beginning of a long journey and during the next chapter, you'll learn how to move a step closer to your dream. Before you start the next chapter, spend a moment thinking about what your mountain and your hike will look like. Think of the people you want to have next to you cheering you on during this journey.

Entrepreneur Jim Rohn put it well: 'Don't take the casual approach to life. Casualness leads to casualties. Seek out the mentors that you need that will lead you to greatness in your field. If you're not willing to learn from others, who are you willing to learn from?'[3]

You have stated what your dreams are and their importance to you. Now, imagine making them happen and who the people are that will stand next to you and help you make them happen.

---

3   Source Forbes: https://www.forbes.com/sites/forbescoachescouncil/2020/09/03/
     the-power-of-mentorship/?sh=30f7fb9f7438.

CHAPTER 4

THE CONFIDENT YOU

Your success will be determined by
the spirit of your actions

*E*verything from now on starts with confidence. *This is what will keep you going.*

Your path towards every achievement is something that you can determine by learning how to shake everything that doesn't serve you and adding skills and tools that will support your aims and help build confidence.

THE FEELING OF STARTING OVER

Once you have reached the base of your mountain and are ready to start your hike, you'll leave your comfort zone behind and will be ready to take on any challenge and obstacle that might come your way.

When I felt the urge to make my next career move, it was a very daunting period as I was in a comfortable place and had worked hard to get there! I had to leave Ashley and Wafa and all the people who were not just colleagues—they had become friends. I was surprised by my desire to change a universe that was peaceful and fulfilling and throw myself into the unknown.

There was a missing element that I could no longer feel—the excitement of being challenged, the excitement of learning new things. In my attempt to resist the urge or maybe amplify it, I decided to start a digital marketing course. Digital marketing was just starting to bloom and I got involved with a few projects where I practised the skills. I joined marketing associations and started to meet people outside my company. At the time, I thought of my actions as a diversion that would satisfy the urge for a challenge but little did I know that all my actions were intended to build my confidence and prepare me for my next move.

THE FEAR OF THE UNKNOWN

But what do you do when you exit that well-known zone that you have worked for? What happens when the people who used to cheer you on are no longer there and are not a few steps away? Where do you find the power to start everything from zero and keep going until you reach a place of total happiness and comfort?

Another very important figure in my life has been my grandfather. Very early in my life, he taught me the beauty of listening to classical music and ballet. I used to think that with two twirls everything could be solved. We listened to Beethoven's 'Moonlight Sonata' and thought of a future filled with happiness, success, health, and hope. Since then, listening to 'Moonlight Sonata' or 'Fur Elise' have helped me clear my mind and find a different perspective on challenges that will keep me going. Beethoven has been a great stimulus for me in finding my way forward.

The months following my decision to find my next career move were hard. The joy of discovering opportunities and thinking of potential new jobs was very soon shattered by multiple rejections. I learned very quickly that waiting for something I wanted was hard. There is enormous pressure that pushes your shoulders down and continuous anxiety prompts a constant question—*what if it does not happen?* You look around you and see that it did happen for other people who, from your perspective, have not worked as much as you and had it very easy.

WHY DOES IT HAVE TO BE
SO HARD FOR YOU?

1. **The feeling of emptiness:** You feel the emptiness of everything you do, disinterest, the lack of energy, the incapacity to do anything. At this point, you are emotionally fighting to get out of this phase, to find a hook that will pull you out. Sometimes, we choose the easiest way out and decide it is okay to go back to where we started. In such moments, I found myself vulnerable to everything around me which becomes superficial and unclear.

2. **The search for new beginnings:** In a few months, the search for a new career opportunity crashed my spirit and self-esteem. On many occasions, I told myself that it was not worth it and I asked myself a million times why I wanted to give up a place of glory for this very challenging journey. But something inside me kept me going—probably my subconscious recognising that I had been on this path before and it led to beautiful things. I assume, though it was buried under layers of disappointment, that my confidence was fighting to come out.

3. **The ugly rejections:** There were many applications, many interviews, and many rejections. Once, I progressed through multiple rounds, and it was a pleasant experience. In the end, I was told that, unfortunately, I had not made it but the company would like to stay in touch and contact me should they have

any additional roles. It was a bittersweet feeling but I was very positive about it. The journey of finding a new career path is not easy and, as my mom once told me, 'Great things are not easy to get.' It takes commitment, resilience, trust in yourself, and belief that what you wish for will eventually happen. There are times when you doubt your abilities and question everything that you have achieved up to that moment and perhaps feel that you are a fraud.

As you think of reaching your next milestone, think of all these moments of desperation when you needed validation for any worthwhile thing that you have done. Write them down.

As you pass these uncomfortable moments, you also get the chance to broaden your universe and get to know different people. Such experiences help you form a realistic picture of the world you wish to enter and prepare you for when you eventually get in.

4. **The experience:** Three months after my interview with the company that asked to stay in touch, I received a call from them inviting me to an interview for a great marketing role. In less than a month I was offered the role and signed the contract. At that point, I achieved a new milestone and positioned myself as ready to embark on the next part of my hike.

The expectations of how this role would support my career and the potential I was imagining matched the image I had when I searched the stars in the sky. Feelings of happiness, accomplishment, and confidence were with me as I drove to work on my first day.

5. **The expectation of new beginnings:** The novelty that I was so craving was there and I had to adjust to a new business environment and different people who challenged my overall understanding of marketing. Here, in this beautiful company, I have taken many of my first steps and, for a very long period, I felt I knew nothing. The more people explained and the more concepts that were introduced, the more I felt there was a huge gap between the expectations of the role and what I brought to the table.

My hunger for change and more responsibility became a struggle for which I was not prepared or thought I was not prepared. After the first month, I wanted to go back to my previous company as, again, the difficulty of the situation made me very uncomfortable. It didn't happen, as people around me understood that I was lost and needed the support that they offered from day one. Hours spent in self-directed research and reading became a normal state for me. Spending time with people and learning about each individual puzzle added value to my day-to-day struggle.

Step by step, mistake by mistake, task by task, in a few months I brought myself to a comfortable space where I could start using my skills and strengths. Finally, the enjoyment and enthusiasm started to return and, once again, I could contribute and bring value.

The next couple of months went very smoothly and everything started to shape up well. However, as I was learning about the company and my role, I realised that there was a focus on graphic execution that was not part of my development vision. This focus somehow grew in its intensity and became a top priority for my management, with my performance being very much linked to this performance indicator. That did not go very well as I had no interest in becoming a graphic designer or developing graphic advertising design skills. And that's when the next struggle began. There was a gap between management expectations and my expectations and there was rejection. But, this time, from my side. I had not signed up for this and my manager found it hard to understand why I could not follow instructions. This is when I experienced the concept of being micromanaged.

It was a tough atmosphere and a constant battle. Everyone was aware of this situation and there were whispers and rolling eyes everywhere, but nobody spoke up to acknowledge the issue. Our marketing team was small at that time. Just four or five people managed multiple projects, which was super challenging and, along with the micromanagement, amounted to a nightmare. We were the first to arrive and the last to leave the office. There was sympathy from people around the organisation and an acknowledgement of our work. But the truth was that everything going out from our desks was top-notch and because of the obsessive attention to detail of my manager, Linda, we always provided high value and great results.

IT IS NOT ALWAYS GLAMOROUS

It was a very stressful period as the organisation was going through a period of massive growth and we had to execute multiple campaigns at any time. I remember one afternoon when we were all slightly behind some hardcore deadlines and the execution was not going as planned. We were frozen at our desks, waiting for something to happen. Linda sat behind us, asking for updates every second, criticising everything we had done that delayed the execution, and blaming every one of us. In such an environment, there was no room for creative thinking, innovative solutions or coming up with a different plan. We were frozen, unable to move, talk, or leave. I remember trying to write an email and not being able to find the words. My brain was overwhelmed by the noise of Linda's questions—I was terrified.

In that moment of total mind and body freeze, something happened. Something inside me gave me the unexpected courage to stand up and say, 'Linda, we all need to calm down. We all need to work this out together and find a different way of making it happen, and you need to stop talking and give us this time.' As I spoke, I looked around me and saw the terrified faces of my colleagues. In a blink of a second, there was fear but also a glimmer of hope.

After I finished this out-of-the-blue intervention, I sat down, somehow waiting for the apocalypse to come. It never came—there was no reaction from Linda. To everyone's surprise, nothing happened. On the contrary, a feeling of calm took over. It came from the release of months of holding on to anger, frustration, and guilt. Overall, there was a sense of relief that I had finally found the confidence to stand up for myself. This event become the subject of many conversations and remains a momentous day in my personal history as, after that, things changed, and Linda became more open to feedback and conversations.

As I think back on that part of my career, I can see that Linda was an outstanding professional with extraordinary talents but these talents and the skill-set she was focused on required people with a graphic design background, which none of us had. And here is where I've learned how difficult the discrepancy can be between expectations and reality. We could never have satisfied

Linda's passion for perfection but we worked hard to do the best we could with the skills we had.

I've never learned how to measure graphics in an advertisement or identify what must be moved one millimetre to the left but, man, oh man, I've learned the importance of attention to detail. I've learned that being frozen in your seat will never be a solution and, most of all, I've learned the benefit of having the courage to speak up. That day, I reinvented myself as a professional and as a leader. Without even realising it, I started a new era for the marketing department.

THE POWER TO KEEP MOVING FORWARD

A few years later, at a gathering of marketers, I had the pleasure of meeting Cristine, the CMO of a well-known multinational. She shared a bit of her experience and one episode stood out for me. It was her continuous struggle to shift and change mindsets, especially those of superiors. Her career story was built on her confidence and daring to change things in the face of any adversity. When she reached middle management and was leading a team, her senior management tasked her to run a global program that had very specific guidelines to attract new customers. After studying the task and discussing it with her team, Cristine realised that it would not work and presented an alternative that she strongly believed would achieve what the company was asking for. Very soon, she understood that her management was not open to alternatives.

Cristine decided to disregard the guidance from her management and go with the option her team, agencies, and other trusted partners had suggested. It was a very bold move. She described many sleepless nights, revisions of action plans, feelings of doubt and guilt, and the fact that her only option was to succeed and overachieve. But her strength was always the confidence and belief she had in her team. The results were stunning and she was thrilled with the performance. However, when her leadership found out that she'd taken a different path, she was demoted to a different function. She was punished for disrespecting the orders of her management.

Word of the results of her campaign and the actions of management reached managers around the organisation and the news spilled into the CEO's office. Soon, she was invited to present the campaign to her CEO and, as a result, she was promoted above her manager. Since that moment, her career has been a success and she became the CMO.

The point is that you need to stand your ground and speak up when things are not going as expected. Another important point relates to expectations and how easy it is to end up in an organisation that you have worked very hard to reach, only to see that there is a huge gap between your expectations and those of management. What do you do? Do you give up as perhaps it is not worth the effort? Do you suffer in silence? Or do you speak up and accept the consequences?

If you now think of your hiking path, what do you do when the track between two milestones is not as expected—the weather forecast changes, your shoes break, or one of your guides gets sick and must return to base? Do you give up and return to base or keep going?

Find shelter from the rain, swap shoes with the guide that must return, and decide to move forward with only one guide.

For this to work, you need to continuously build your confidence.

Confidence is a skill that you build over years and with experience. It is a double-edged sword. You build confidence mostly when you are outside your comfort zone and undertaking new actions but you first need the confidence to say yes to things that take you outside your comfort zone. The confident you will keep going through everything and provide guidance through dark days.

Building your confidence and moving forward will lead you to discover your purpose, understand who you are as a person, and discover your unique skills and values.

CHAPTER 5

THE PERSONAL LEADERSHIP PARADIGM

Your unique talents and personality are
what will help thrive in dark

Back at school, I always struggled with maths. It was not something I was good at or had any interest in. When I was twelve, I started private classes three times a week. It was a real struggle for me and, to make it worse, there were high expectations of good marks and a belief that if you were not good at maths, you had no future.

My parents did everything possible to help, but my results were not as good as expected. After a year, around the time I turned fourteen, it became a real nightmare, with many hours of study allocated to a subject I hated. This continued until one day my parents were called to the school to discuss my mediocre performance in the subject. You see, my family was well-known and there were expectations that I should be an A student. At that meeting, the teacher committee blamed my parents for not focusing enough on my maths improvement and blamed and shamed me for not putting in enough effort. I'm sure you can imagine how I felt. I wanted to disappear under the desk while the discussion went on and on.

After listening to a storm of unrealistic comments, my mom stood up and said that from that moment on she would cancel my extracurricular maths sessions her only expectation would be for me to do the minimum.

I have the image of her standing up not only to my school leadership but to a society poisoned by mediocracy, where talents and uniqueness are not recognised. In front of the teacher committee, she turned to me and apologised for making me go through that ordeal. She said, from that moment on she would focus on the skills that made me unique and extraordinary.

As women, we are always attending to everyone and everything else and forget to focus on what makes us unique. We forget our passions and hobbies. We have very little time to think about who we are as individuals and reflect on our life journeys.

This chapter will be helping you re-evaluate the person you are and guide you towards finding your purpose. It will be a self-discovery of your inner drive toward making things possible and understanding how dreams can be realised when they are connected to purpose.

THE POWER OF SELF-CREATED INTERNAL BATTLES AND HOW YOU CAN SUCCEED

Everyone's career journey is made up of unique moments that build up over time through multiple dreams, desires, and actions. Realising where we want to go depends on our self-discovery.

We make plans from childhood about what we want to become without having any real basis for our ideas. Every day, all around you, there are conversations taking place in which kids are being asked what they want to be when they are older. Their answers are always related to their talents and passions. But you also hear adults joking about their kids' answers and eight times out of ten their underlying expectations are for kids to become doctors, lawyers, or teachers—whatever professions the parents believe to be valuable or honourable.

I also have such conversations with my children and now my daughter is keen to become a scientist and study at Oxford, while my son wants to be a basketball player and study at MIT. These are genuine dreams that as a parent I will support and I will guide my children toward making them happen. But I also know that their dreams may change and new ideas might emerge.

As we grow up and enter the workforce, our genuine desires and dreams might be exchanged for convenience and comfort as we conform to social pressure. In most cases, when asked about what they want, women will say, 'I don't know,' which often translates to, 'I have lost my way.'

THE WOMAN IN THE MIRROR

My friend, Cecille, is a very talented pianist who in her early twenties received multiple international awards for her music and was recognised as being among the top twenty international pianists. But Cecille decided to give up her musical career to start a family. She married in her late twenties and had three children who she adores. She is a joyful and grateful person and her life has been dedicated to raising and supporting the family. But on this journey, like many of us, she lost the spark and believes she has lost qualities that made her unique. In multiple conversations, Cecille admitted that she didn't know who she was anymore and the role of being a mom and wife was no longer enough.

Like Cecille, for a few years as my children were growing, I put many of my dreams on hold. It was a personal decision that I took due to those familiar feelings of guilt, fear of being selfish, and societal expectations. I've never given up on my career but it got deprioritised. A few years ago, my daughter asked me, 'Mom, what do you like? What are your hobbies?' I said tennis, reading, and travelling. And she said, 'But are you doing any of them?' *That was a turning point for me. My four-year-old daughter was questioning the person her mom was.* That conversation has changed my entire journey to the point that I've started taking tennis classes and playing in competitions and, as you can see, I've decided to write a book.

Cecille has not returned yet to her music career and continues to try to be the best mom she can be. I asked her once if she thinks back to her successful days as a professional pianist. She said, 'That is the past and no longer possible. I must focus on the present and my children.'

How do you make such decisions? Where do you find the strength to give up the person you are and have worked to become and dedicate yourself to a new life, a new version of you?

I think of myself as a lucky person as I was blessed with open-minded parents who have educated me to know how to make the right decisions and taught me that only by working hard can I accomplish my dreams. They have also put my personal needs and dreams ahead of everything. Since then, my husband has become my biggest supporter in everything I want to achieve and my equal partner in life.

Such positive environments have helped me to focus on my growth and development without being forced to conform to social pressure. I always had the opportunity to choose my actions based on the person I wanted to become. This has helped me build a kit of strong personal values and ethics that support my actions.

Still, like many women, I have had moments when I lost myself. Here are some key insights that helped me return to myself.

THE INGREDIENTS OF
YOUR PARADIGM

Since the beginning of my career, I have probably done over a thousand interviews, and one question stood out from them all: 'Where do you see yourself in five years?' In the beginning, I thought of it as a cliché, a must-ask question to which you don't prepare an answer as one would come on the spot. The truth is that this question has somehow guided my career to date. It gave me a scope and an objective to steer my actions toward making things happen.

As you think of your hiking journey, write down the events that have happened in your life and career over the last five years:

As part of my five-year journey, I have:

- Joined a new company
- Changed to a completely different industry and started working with new people
- Been promoted and given a wider geographical area to manage and more responsibility as a people manager
- Started a new hobby, playing tennis
- Gone through a company restructure, moved to a different team, became a single contributor, lost my direct reports, and started an MBA in Leadership, Innovation and Change
- Moved to a different line of business with a 300% increase in revenue
- Become a certified practitioner in diversity and inclusion
- Been promoted to a global role
- Since joining the new company, visited multiple countries and been to my home country more often

- Bought a house after fifteen years of living in Dubai, changed cars and moved kids to a different school
- Changed jobs again in 2017, after going through thirty interviews and rejections before starting this brand-new chapter
- Lost the 9 to 5 office hours and had to learn how to organise myself
- Developed a morning routine with a 5 am start to accommodate everything on my to-do list
- Undertaken many business trips of 24-48 hours with overnight flights to be home in the morning and take my children to school
- Worked multiple late-evening hours once my family went to sleep to develop my leadership skills
- Prioritised learning and development in my life—some would say my life was divided into three pillars: family, work, and study

And the list keeps going. *What is important to note is that while I have seen great success, there have also been many hours of hard work and compromise. During this period, I have learned self-leadership and how to direct my efforts, feelings, and emotions towards a positive goal.*

When I was offered the chance for a promotion, I saw it as the ultimate milestone and the biggest career achievement I could imagine. Achieving my dream of what the future could be reflected all of my efforts toward that moment.

The journey started with a conversation with my manager, who was a keen supporter of me as a professional and very keen to help me embark on this new journey. In a matter of a few months, there were several managerial changes and a new leadership team was appointed.

During this time, I was asked to cover a role on an interim basis in addition to my usual role. They were a challenging few months—multiple projects running at the same time, new leadership, and additional stakeholders—which translated into double the hours of work. Every day, additional tasks and projects were added to my to-do list and I accepted it all from a fear of failure and being seen as not ready to take over the leadership position. I started work at 6 am and finished around 11:30 pm. I couldn't leave home without my laptop and worked from the tennis court while my daughter played, at the cinema while my family watched a movie, in the car, on holiday, and when I visited my parents.

My anxiety grew higher and higher. I snapped at my children and lost sight of my passion and, after a few months, developed health problems. *But I was able to justify it as being for what I thought of as a higher purpose—it was for something I wanted so badly.* This beautiful picture that I created was crushed when the newly appointed senior management considered that I was not qualified for the position. They were looking for somebody with experience in the top Fortune companies.

MAKING SENSE OF REJECTIONS

It was a rejection I was not prepared for. After being told that I was not chosen for the role, I believe my heart stopped. I couldn't feel anything. I was mentally and physically frozen. I experienced a mix of emotions that included hate, frustration, disappointment, guilt, and pain. I felt like I was having a nightmare and wanted to wake up. People around me were shocked and sad and empathised.

To my surprise, in a few days, I was back on my feet and decided to look at the entire experience as a moment of growth in my career. There were moments when all I wanted to do was give up and get out of there. But my confidence and deep values unexpectedly kicked in and gave me the strength to go on. After days of self-reflection on the drivers that created that unfortunate situation, I decided to make changes and put structure into my own life. While I decided to move on and act as interim manager, I also established boundaries and declined tasks and projects that fell outside these boundaries.

Balancing work and family became a priority and in a very short time, I felt free of the negative feelings I had carried. For the first time, I hired a coach who successfully guided and supported me through this period. His main teaching centred on being able to see everything from a different perspective and positioning this incident as one moment on my journey of identifying my purpose. As I was recovering my balance and bringing back positivity while searching for things that would fulfil me as a person, I was invited to a leadership meeting to represent marketing. It was surprising and unexpected.

I called one of my mentors who had prepared me for this position and asked him what I should do. He gave me one line: 'Act as a leader.' And I did. *My participation was extraordinary to the point that after a few conversations with all managers present, I was back to being considered for the role and, after a few weeks, I was appointed as manager.*

THE DISCOVERED FOLLOW-UP

When I look back over the years, I can recognise that this one key moment of my life has been a cornerstone for my growth and development as a professional. It was a moment of intense feelings that I managed to channel to my benefit. The learnings of this episode have been enormous and, somehow now looking back, I am grateful for going through that experience as it added new strength to my confidence and moved me on to the next hiking milestone of my journey.

We go through life with the opportunity to make choices—choices that define our lives and us as people. It is we who decide how much ownership we take over events and how much we let family, friends, and society be involved. It is in our core values and confidence that we find the strength to keep going.

What I've learned from this and other episodes is that when we find ourselves at a crossroads, we are ready to make changes. When we find ourselves in the darkest moments of our lives, we find the strength to move on and make dramatic changes. I would have loved to be able to anticipate such moments and make necessary changes before it was too late.

Gary, the coach I have worked with throughout this time, showed me the importance of staying connected to my higher aim and supported me in finding my ultimate purpose. In my naïve mind, I thought that working hard must be the ultimate goal. Once in the right state of mind, it is easier to navigate through challenges and make comebacks for better results. Through his coaching, I've learned how to use my powers to drive alignment with what I am in this life to do.

This leads us into the next chapter, where I will talk about my journey to find and understand my purpose and the impact this has had on my leadership and career growth. It will also teach you how to discover your own purpose.

CHAPTER 6

DEFINING YOU

When your goals and desires are
connected to the definition of you

THE JOURNEY OF FINDING YOUR HIGHEST VOCATION

*H*ave you ever been asked what your purpose is and been expected to immediately come up with the aim of your existence? You try to squeeze your feelings and your mind to come up with a statement that summarises your life. I don't know about you, but when asked this question, I would try to dig deep and think of what I valued most in life, what I was good at, and what my passions were. This trial of self-discovery would go on for a few minutes and, because it was an impossible task, my mind would start to play tricks on me and send messages like, *This task is unrealistic and impossible.*

Maybe some of you have managed to articulate a clear vision of who you are. Well done! I believe this is probably one of the biggest achievements. As for the rest of us, well, most of us are *still seeking the highest understanding of our individual existences.*

In much of the training I have completed, I was told that purpose should not be related to work. This seems misleading to me as we spend half of our time each day working. I've always felt that the projects, tasks, and people that I have a responsibility to must be related to my purpose.

Could purpose be our heart's desire at any point in time and finding a way to thrive through the storms to make it happen?

Two years after I got married to the most wonderful man on earth, we were ready to start a family. The happiness of the moment we made that decision, the idea of becoming a mother, was unexpected and beautiful. *What I wanted carried a very high spiritual meaning for me.*

I wanted to be a mother and become the best mother I could be—the rest didn't count. And I had a gorgeous little girl. My maternity leave was rather short—a bit over three months—and when I went back to work, I left my daughter in the care of a nanny. While I felt slightly devastated and missed her every single second during the first week, somehow I was happy to be back at work and restarting my career journey. *What happened to my purpose? Was I selfish right there in that moment?*

Many judgemental voices questioned my decision and added pressure to the weight I already carried. But it didn't matter as my focus was on resettling into the corporate world—as a mother, this time—and finding a new balance that would work for me and my family.

My journey into motherhood was a learning curve. I started with little knowledge and support. Living in a different country to my and my husband's family as new parents gave us no choice but to 'make it happen.' And we did. We now have two beautiful children aged ten and twelve who have brought us the most wonderful times of our lives. And while *'family is everything'* might sound like a cliché, it truly is the foundation of our success, our future, and our society.

THE POWER OF MINDSET CHANGE

But motherhood and a happy family have always been just a part of my journey. As my children grew and became more independent, I prepared for my next career jump. The truth is that the nine months of pregnancy, the maternity leave, and the first years of my kids' lives had put everything on hold. Sadly, we still live in a society that sees maternity as a barrier to multiple aspects of life. There is this idea that maternity changes you as a person and that while you experience it your performance drops and, unofficially, you are not entitled to promotions or bonuses.

The sad thing for me was that I accepted that. I bowed in front of society and said it was okay for my career to take a step back as I would have more time to focus on my baby. This unfair mindset that I accepted is something that I am now motivated to fight against so that my daughter will have a different experience.

One of my Romanian friends, Andy, a well-known news presenter, also went back to work three months after the birth of her baby, even though Romania allowed twelve months of maternity leave. The judgement she received was astonishing and most observers believed that she would lose her job or be taken off prime-time news. But Andy went back into her role right from the start and, in the blink of an eye, found that balance between career and children.

Another friend of mine, Letti, decided to take a longer break from work and focus on raising her child. Her decision was fully supported by her husband and family but, of course, voices around her were whispering that she had no ambitions or desires.

Why does it have to be like this? Many of us have children and choose to have different motherhood experiences. The choice must belong to us. We shouldn't shy away from a promotion because we are expecting a baby. We shouldn't feel guilty as we go back to work and our children are home. And we shouldn't feel shame if we decide to stay home permanently to raise our family. Maternity leave and the decision to have children should be complementing our lives, not putting them on pause.

While society and many organisations have taken steps towards a more inclusive culture, it is hard to see that we, as women, must still deal with stereotypes and events that diminish our status as professionals and mothers.

My friend, Reem, was told that before going on maternity leave she must find her replacement and was asked to take weekly calls while on leave. She was told that her role was not guaranteed upon her return and that she might have to take on a different role. Why are these conversations still happening?

I've heard about many such experiences and I'm sure you have too, and it breaks my heart. It fills me with frustration and fuels my desire to do something about it. So, if you are a mother and reading my book, I want you to write down your maternity story and send it to me. *Let's bring together a community that shares stories and has the power to change things and create a better world for our daughters. Right here, I have shared with you my purpose.*

Like many of you, I have been completely changed by motherhood. Overnight, I became responsible for another soul, another human being. While, in the beginning, it was more about the child's primary needs, I soon realised that this responsibility was about creating a better future, leaving a legacy, and becoming a role model, as well as leading myself to a place of self-achievement. For me, this achievement was coming from a continuous thrust to develop and keep a growth mindset. I didn't take motherhood as a replacement for everything else and the highest status I could achieve. I took it as another part of what defines me as a woman. And I tried to blend it into my life without forgetting the person I had been before motherhood.

As women, we must have the freedom to choose what is right for us and what defines us. We need to work together to drop the nasty judgement that comes with every situation. When I was eight months pregnant, I went out for dinner with friends. The conversation touched on my very pregnant status and if I would return to work. When I said yes, I would return to work because work is part of who I am, one of the men said that when he was a child, his mom stayed at home to provide her children with cooked food and that is what he wanted for his children as well. I don't know if his comment was just an opinion, as my husband said later, but it felt like a strong judgement. I felt angry and wanted to comment on such an insult, but didn't. I felt people have the right to an opinion and to share different values and beliefs, and that I could decide which opinions I wanted to support. We finished the dinner quicker than anyone expected and it was the last time we saw that couple.

I salute diversity and respect different opinions and points of view. What I don't like, and reject, is when these ideas are imposed as best practice.

BUILDING A STRONGER FUTURE TOGETHER

I've decided to write a book as part of my purpose as I have often felt that *ordinary people like me and you can influence each other to fight battles, thrive through society's pressures, walk through the dark moments, and reach the light.* I am a very simple person from a little town in Romania who has found the confidence to hike and learn how to always move towards achievement. *I want to share my story because I believe with everything I have that when you want something, you can achieve it.*

I want each one of you to share your stories and influence others. Together, we have this unbelievable power to strike out and create change. My purpose is to offer my children a better future which I have contributed to making.

I've learned that purpose is something that evolves with every experience, positive and negative, that you live through.

It is something that defines you as a person and brings together all your skills and passions. It is that motivation that will keep you going through the dark moments, through moments of desperation and doubt. It is what defines you at work, at home, and every-where. I loved the answer a senior executive gave when asked, 'How do you balance your work with personal life?' She said, 'I only have one life—I don't have one personal life and one work life. *My main goal every day I wake up is to do the best I can in every second of my one life.*'

When you get that 'what is your purpose question' and need to come up with an answer, don't pressure yourself—you will not find it.

As you are juggling your way through your journey and trying to fit everything in, it's important to understand that as you evolve and grow as a person, your aspirations and desires will change and become more meaningful.

THE INFLUENCE PEOPLE HAVE OVER YOU

During my professional life, I have met several leaders that have influenced and guided my career in the most creative and beneficial ways. *These people are standing at your crossroads and guide you towards the direction you want to take. They are the ones who will believe in you and stand with you, no matter what, and will be there for you in your most challenging moments.* I also have met leaders that would bring no value to your growth. On the contrary, they would suck all your energy and turn your positive creativity into a wall of doubt and low self-esteem, leaving you unable to recognise yourself as a person.

A few months after I returned to work after having my second child, a gorgeous boy, I was given the opportunity to work for a different company in a role with several key responsibilities. I was recommended to the hiring manager by a mutual friend and the recruitment process was quick. I am not sure if my manager's respect for me was somehow hindered by the speed with which I was hired but from day one, she was not my advocate. She didn't mind using the kind of manipulation, humiliation, and micromanaging techniques that will transform you into the most miserable person.

I remember days when I was sitting at my desk in an absolute brain fog as there was no stimulus to keep me going. She was the kind of leader who always felt superior to everything and everyone, who would enjoy humiliating jokes aimed at my nationality or my husband's nationality, and who would take no ownership of her actions. In many conversations I had with colleagues, HR, and her superiors, I was told 'you just have to get to know her better' and 'she is very good at what she is doing and is well-connected' or 'she is a very nice person, just has a bit too much ego.'

Thinking back, I remember trying very hard to be a person I was not to connect with her. In these moments of desperation, I forgot who I was and what my purpose was and tried to lose myself to gain her approval.

By doing that, I subconsciously decided that she was right, that it was my fault everything was going badly, and that perhaps I was not qualified for the job. Such situations don't last long and, sooner than you think, you will find a way to get out of these constraints. In my case, the universe decided to move me to a different manager after a company restructure. It was a new beginning, an opportunity to do my job and enhance my professional life. This episode became very valuable, as it showed me what I never want to be, especially after I became a people manager.

The learning that I received was that being difficult and trying to dominate and manipulate people is something that will bring satisfaction to some. But facing up to these behaviours makes you a stronger person and builds your confidence. Being strong and moving away from this kind of behaviour is a sign of maturity and understanding that the world is much bigger than one small angry person. Such situations create very strong bonds with colleagues as you share the same dramas and learn how to open up to each other. You will share every tear and smile and, most of all, you'll be there for each other. Some of my strongest friendships happened right there and I am grateful for having the opportunity to meet those people. Although we stopped working together years ago when I moved to a different organisation, we still enjoy the same positive vibes and connection as we did when we saw each other every day.

YOUR STORY MUST BE WRITTEN BY YOU

My personal belief is that each day, with each new experience, you add a new angle to what defines you as a person and your goals. These goals can be anything you want, anything that is important than you as a person, but they must be something that you have chosen without constraints, societal or financial pressure, guilt, or from trying to meet somebody else's expectations.

Reading this book means that you have decided to take this hike with me and are on the way or already reaching the top of the mountain. This is the time for you to think about how you have reached this decision and why this mountain is important to you.

What is your mountain top?

_____

_____

_____

_____

_____

_____

_____

_____

_____

The top of my mountain would probably carry the name of my daughter as since her birth she has been my muse and motivation for everything I have done. While many things have changed as I have moved toward the top, there has always been a main thread—making or influencing change based on my strong desire to make a better world for my daughter.

Being able to articulate and visualise your purpose doesn't mean things will get easier or you will have a clear path. On the contrary, the closer you are to reaching a goal, a milestone, the top of a mountain, or the top of a second or third mountain, the more stressful and difficult it can become. You will have to fight your fights and walk the path you've chosen. You will make mistakes and rectify them. You will grow and develop. And each day you will get closer to your highest goal. Knowing your purpose, what motivates and inspires you, will guide you through your darkest moments and give you the strength and power to overcome all obstacles.

Along your journey, there will be supportive people who you will cherish and keep close to your heart and there will also be people who cause you suffering and pain. But everyone will teach you a lesson and give you strength and additional power.

My journey has been filled with beautiful women who have had a great impact on the person I am today. There is a clear need to be surrounded by such people who have a clear understanding of their mission in life and offer you a hand when you are in need.

As we continue creating your hiking track, I want you to think of people who have had a different point of view to you. How have you reacted? What did you do? Are these people still part of your trusted group?

CHAPTER 7

WOMEN SUPPORTING WOMEN

A few years back during a leadership workshop, I was asked to build a map of people—friends, mentors, and colleagues—who have had a true impact on my professional life. The objective of the exercise was to send thank you notes to each one of them. I didn't notice at the time, but ninety per cent of the people who made a real impact on my career were women. Each milestone for me is somehow connected to an incredible woman who stood by me and offered unconditional support.

While each of these amazing humans is from a different corner of the world, there is one thing that connects us—the force within us that makes us believe that with effort, self-discipline, ambition, and desire, everything is possible.

Seeing the strength of cherishing such connections probably started with my mom.

MY MOM, THE PERSON I ALWAYS WANTED TO BECOME

My mom, a woman of many talents, *with an unbeatable desire to succeed*, has always been my compass in life. While managing a successful career and looking after a family of two children—me and my brother—without any help, she created a fairy-tale picture that showed women can achieve anything. Her energy, passion, and love can be seen in everything she touched. She has been retired for a few years but remains the most energetic woman I know. To this day, she continues to bring that sort of spark and exuberance.

There are so many memories linked to her magic but Christmas stands out as the most wonderful time in our house and not because of the presents, but because of the atmosphere that my mom created. The smell of her baking combined with the smell of the freshly cut Christmas tree and the sight of the snow outside is what I call magic.

For many years, we were cut off from gas cooking facilities during the daytime and all the Christmas magic happened at night. After dinner and putting us to sleep, my mom would spend the night baking, cooking, and decorating. In the early morning, before waking us up, she would make breakfast and greet us with a big smile before going to work. Everything looked so smooth and effortless, even though I know she must have been so tired. To us, she was a superwoman who could achieve just about anything.

And this is exactly the type of lesson my mom wanted to teach me. A superwoman can do everything she wants but works hard to create the magic.

I remember at one point she was given the opportunity to take a second job part-time. She took it, but at no moment did my brother and I feel less attention from her. Even now, I don't know how she juggled everything but she did it with flying colours. She believed that when an opportunity comes your way, it is easy to say no and find reasons for not being able to accomplish things. But that is a waste of your life. For her, a lack of time was never an excuse to say no and her philosophy was that to be successful in life you must focus on your strengths and keep developing them.

She also had a network of women who supported each other and developed generations of workers in her field. There is an enormous gratitude that she receives from the team members she has mentored. Her empathy, diplomacy, diligence, and self-leadership have made her a role model for many generations of women and the template for the superwoman that I aspire to be.

Having such a strong figure in my life has subconsciously given me the power to thrive.

THE POWER OF NETWORKS

I've always looked to be *surrounded by people who share similar values and beliefs* as me. I am not sure if the law of attraction has played a role, but many of the people who have different sets of values have been somehow removed from my path. The second part of the exercise that I mentioned at the beginning of this chapter was to think of the people who you have met but are no longer part of your life and think about the reasons behind this.

As you are envisioning your hiking track, I am giving you an imaginary map and encouraging you to write down the people who have supported you up to now and the people who you have removed from your path. Who can you see?

A few years ago, just after I joined a new company, I met Alia. We were both new to the team and our roles and, together, we started a new adventure that quickly transformed our relationship into a strong friendship. Alia and I came from different backgrounds and different experiences—she was more than ten years younger than me—but our differences were superficial as we both shared the drive to be successful.

I think Alia would agree that this was one of the most successful times of our professional lives. And it happened because, with every step we took, we had each other. The trust, confidence, and chemistry we built was so powerful that it kept us going, successfully knocking down challenge after challenge.

One of the most successful marketing activities that we've run together took place in Athens and, one month before the kick-off, we were sent to visit the venue and work out the customer journey. Once in Athens, after visiting a few gorgeous locations and finalising the agenda, we sat down and looked at each other and whispered, 'We need to make this work.'

At that time, we had no customer registrations for the event or confirmed speakers. The next four weeks were chaotic, to say the least. We worked twenty hours a day, calling and inviting customers, confirming speakers, even working on graphics—but it had to be done. We used to bring two sets of clothes to work and order food at the office. Bathroom breaks were a luxury.

In the end, it turned out to be an incredible success. We had a small team supporting us and little budget but the magic was created by our infectious energy and attitude. To us, nothing was impossible, and our energy and attitude gave us an influence within the company that has opened many doors for us.

CONFIDENCE AND TRUST BRING YOU THE DESIRED SUCCESS

It took me longer than expected to write this chapter as I was going through some unexpected personal situations (that might become a subject for my next book!). Life really doesn't stop throwing you curveballs, hey! It was a busy time at work with many deadlines and projects that I was not able to focus on for a few days.

And this is where the power of true friendship kicked in. My very new colleague, Sophie, took over all my work without hesitation and just rolled with it. Not for a moment did she worry that her working hours would become much longer, that her family would see very little of her, or that she might just fail. *She knew that in that moment I needed her and she had to be there for me.* And that's the true value of friendship—when you need someone's help, that person is there for you.

A few months after I returned to work after having my second child, I was feeling overwhelmed and unable to manage all the tasks in front of me. We were at a conference and, by coincidence, I met one of the people I admire most—Lama, the CEO of a local company who had four children, an impeccable body, and who was and all-around genius. When I saw her, I tried to hide as I was still struggling with baby weight and feeling tired and had black circles under my eyes.

She saw me and came from the VIP area of the conference to greet me. I don't think I was able to articulate two words, but I felt tears coming down my cheek and was unable to stop them. She hugged me and asked to meet after the conference. I couldn't face seeing her and decided to leave the conference and send her a quick message that I had an emergency and had to go home. I felt weak and vulnerable. I felt like a coward.

Lama called me a week later to check on the emergency and again invited me for lunch. This time, I went, and I told her that I had left the conference because I was unable to face the image of perfection that she represents when I couldn't cope with two children and a middle-level job. Lama knew that it was an excuse but she didn't know why, and she pulled out her phone to show me a photo of her return to work after having her second child. She was still wearing her maternity clothes and had been only a manager at that time.

Lama's advice that afternoon was that we, as women, need to have a network of inspiring women who will support us through our transformation. After that day, for almost a year, we met weekly for lunch. Every time, she would bring one of her friends, each with a different story. The challenges they shared turned out to have practical and easy solutions, but they confirmed that things can feel so hard when you are overwhelmed. From Lama and her friends, I've learned that it is okay to be in a situation, but it is important to have a plan of action if you wish to make changes. Lama always said to me, 'Life is about choices, which sooner or later will define the person you are.' At the end of that year, I managed to drop all the post-baby weight by going to the gym. My first child went to nursery three times a week, giving me a bit more free time, and I was ready for my next career move.

LIFE IS ABOUT CHOICES

There isn't a recipe for success but, as Lama said, 'life is about choices,' and I will add 'with determination and ambition, you must make things happen.' When speaking to women, sometimes I hear 'yes, but it is easy for you' or 'you were very lucky.' Nothing is easy, and I wouldn't put luck very high up on my opportunities scale. The choices I have made throughout my life have allowed me to embrace opportunities and get through the challenges I have faced.

The choices I have made about who to accept as part of my life have played an important role in my success. There isn't an easy path or, at least, I didn't find it. And this is the lesson I want to pass on to my daughter, who has given me the strength to start and finish the book. I want to create a better world where gender is no longer something that is discussed in business conversations and inner equality is more than a concept. I also want her to know that achieving her dreams is possible if she work hard, and I want to teach her how to make the right choices in life, especially when it comes to people. I want to pass on the confidence that my mom passed to me, that she is a superwoman and nothing is stopping her from achieving her dreams.

There are many people we meet, many people who connect with us, but only a few will become part of our lives. I have always believed chemistry and sharing similar values are components that help me choose the people I want to be part of my career and my life. A few years ago, I was running a big project at the organisation I was working at. To support me with the project, I invited a few agencies to pitch, and that is when I met Hana. She was leading a boutique agency and was super excited to be given the opportunity to work with me.

However, her pitch did not meet my expectations and she wasn't awarded the project. I was straightforward about my disappointment and frustration and she took my feedback with a brave face. After this project was complete, she reconnected with me and wanted to get to know me better and understand my personality. Somewhere in my heart, I felt connected to her and decided to meet up. Hana was very interested in getting to know more about my background, my values in life, and my goals. That same year, I called agencies for a different project and was impressed to see Hana's presentation was spot-on. She was awarded the project and many more to come.

Hana has become an extension of my team and has offered unconditional support through multiple challenging moments.

Through her very hard work and ambition to provide the absolute best services, she has helped me to successfully progress through my career. The projects we have run together have been applauded around the organisations and opened unexpected opportunities for me.

Hind, a fearless and inspirational executive that I admire has witnessed many of the projects I have run in partnership with Hana. For Hind, what Hana and I created has become a benchmark whose standards he asks everyone to meet. When Hind changed roles and was promoted, she recommended me for a great role, which I was awarded.

My experience has taught me that once you find people who make a difference to your life, you must keep them close to your heart and cherish them for the rest of your life. I consider myself a very blessed person as I was given the opportunity to meet several wonderful women. Now, look at your map and see who the people in your network are and how they have made an impact on your life. Send a thank you to the ones who you wish to continue being in touch with and delete the ones who have hurt you. They no longer belong to your circle.

I loved the article written by Shelley Zalis, 'Power of the Pack: Women Who Support Women are More Successful.'[4] Shelley rightly said, 'A woman alone has power; collectively we have impact. Traditionally we have been taught to be competitive with one another because there was such a scarcity of jobs at the top. It's so clear that strategy doesn't work. The truth is that raising each other up and channelling the power of collaboration is truly how

---

4   Source: https://www.forbes.com/sites/shelleyzalis/2019/03/06/power-of-the-pack-women-who-support-women-are-more-successful/?sh=a34594f1771a.

we'll change the equation—and have a lot more fun along the way.'

Women that supported you

_____

_____

_____

_____

_____

_____

_____

_____

CHAPTER 8
THE FINAL STRETCH

By now, you should know my life and career story well. For a long time, I had not considered the idea of writing a book, especially after I was told that journalism and writing are not for me, and I almost got fired for my poor English. But here I am, writing the final chapter of my book!

And where are you? Do you have an imaginary top of the mountain that you wish to reach? If you have followed the hiking track that I have guided you along, you should be somewhere close. I found out that setting a goal is not easy. Knowing what you want is not something that you will discover overnight.

For me, the final stretch started with receiving negative news on a promotion that I was very much looking for, a promotion that I had worked for over many years and considered mine. The news came while I was on holiday with my family and, I must admit, it crushed my universe. It was one of those moments when something you believe in and work for doesn't happen and you ask yourself, 'Where do I go from here? How did I not see this coming? How was I so blind in believing so strongly in something? How could I fail?' And although deep down, you know that something else will come along, you can't stop yourself from feeling shame and guilt and wondering where you went wrong and what you could have done better.

It is that moment of being at a crossroads when you need to take a deep breath and find the power to pull yourself up and start again from the beginning. Finding the power to make a fresh start has always led me to unexpected, wonderful experiences.

I don't know if the energy comes from curiosity about new adventures or the desire to hide from painful experiences, but it has always helped me to stand up and move on.

The failure to be appointed to that job motivated me to think of something new. I remember sitting with my husband on the balcony of our hotel, looking at the blue sea and telling him: 'I want to write a book. I want to do something that will make a difference, even a small one. I want women to know that success is possible with hard work and perseverance. And we all have a story and should find the voice to tell it.'

I knew nothing about writing a book, but I had the enormous privilege to meet an amazing book coach who helped to make it happen. Clare cheered me up and was there to put me back on my hiking track when I strayed off it.

There are many moments in our lives when we feel cheated, when we feel that unfair actions have been taken against us. But I want you to find the power to stand up and be okay to start a new journey. The sense of novelty and being outside your comfort zone will open unknown doors for you and bring unexpected adventures that will help you reach the top of your mountain. By reading this book, you should have discovered some of the opportunities and challenges that you have ahead of you and the strength of your base, which you can always come back to when in need. You are now ready to take your next step and make your dreams possible.

I have written this book from my desire to show women like me that reaching the top of imaginary mountains is possible, and that we all have a story and can learn from each other. In many of my conversations with Clare, I expressed doubt that my life story would be of interest to anyone. But Clare would relate my story to her own stories and those of her friends and we could see how inspiring and authentic real-life stories are. As women, we share many journeys and this shared experience supports us through life. While writing the book, I am finishing an MBA with a major in leadership and my thesis is about women in leadership. The gender gap in leadership remains wide and social and cultural stereotypes remain an obstacle for women leaders. Organisations are making progress in closing this gap and supporting women and we need to be ready and prepared to jump on board with this momentum.

This is a great opportunity for you to take the next step in your career. Listen to your inner voice and start working on your next move.

On many occasions, due to high work requirements, I found myself not coping with life. Sometimes, there was an unwritten expectation that you must be connected to the internet for sixteen or seventeen hours a day to demonstrate your efficiency. Meetings were scheduled back-to-back, with people eating lunch and dinner in front of their screens. All while children were home doing online schooling.

It was an absolute struggle to deal with feelings of guilt and frustration while trying to multitask and adapt, and it didn't go well for me. I had to speak up and share my struggles with my colleagues. I knew that everyone was suffering but I was not expecting them to echo and support my views. As we've learned together how to navigate the unknown, we've also learned how to organise ourselves and support each other. It was, again, a moment of finding my voice and speaking up.

Having the confidence to speak up and make bold decisions has been my breakthrough and an unparalleled experience. My parents have taught me the power of being confident and how to be strong, work hard, and follow my dreams. I married a man who shares the same values and principles as me—he has become my rock and shows me unconditional support for every single action I take. My friends and the people I have remained close to have a similar mindset: *always move forward and don't stop until you have achieved your highest goal.* And this is my personal force that allows me to thrive through the challenges and make things happen.

I have always believed that every person you meet, and every experience you live through, is there to teach you a lesson and lead you somewhere. Many of these people or experiences will disconnect from you when they no longer play an active part in your life. Some of them might harm you and create frustration and disappointment and I encourage you to let those people go. This will make room for new, amazing, and sometimes unexpected things that will lead to success. I couldn't have made it here without the amazing women who have supported me on my career journey. I am not sure why they have chosen to guide me, but I will be forever grateful.

I hope my book has inspired you to steer your life and career in the direction of your dreams. Go back to the place you came from and revisit the dreams that ten-year-old girls have. They might not become one hundred per cent reality, but they'll show you the right direction. I have not become an actress or a journalist but here I am, writing the final chapter of my first book. Every step I have taken has led to this unexpected, unconventional outcome: me becoming an author and having the confidence to share my career story with you.

I have reached the top of my mountain and am looking forward to my next hiking trip to a higher peak.

Pain, frustration, and disappointment are all part of the journey and will teach you something. You just need to be open to making adjustments and trust yourself. Over the years, I have learned and developed many skills but something that I treasure and has helped me to this point is being confident and patient. The bigger the goals are, the more patience you need to have.

I used to find statements like 'you are the owner of your life; you can choose what to do next' very cliché. It is such an easy thing to say, but how can it happen when nothing in front of you presents an opportunity? Everything is dark and you are trapped in a vicious cycle. It takes time, but once you find a way to break this cycle, the light will come in and new beginnings will start to show themselves. Don't be afraid to make changes. Don't be afraid to leave what is toxic behind. You deserve the chance to be happy and find your purpose.

CONCLUSION

Here we are at the end of a journey together—or perhaps I should say the beginning of your new journey. I hope that while reading the previous pages, you have found some key insights to confidence and self-leadership and have created a clear mental picture of the top of your mountain. Most of all, I hope you enjoyed the ride.

This is just the first step of your transformation. As you progress through the ups and downs of life, I hope you take with you the five main lessons:

- Find your dream and your vision
- Be confident
- Be agile when choosing people to ride with you
- Know your purpose
- Embrace and share the support of your network of women

Now you should embrace the moment and celebrate the vision of the person you wish to become. You have taken the most difficult step—you have dared to be brave and are prepared to change to become the person of your dreams.

Now it is time to start planning your journey. I would love to hear from you, so leave me a comment at biancazenkel.com, and I'll get back to you.

I'm proud of you! Now go and make a life you can be proud of.

Bianca Zenkel

ACKNOWLEDGMENTS:

I would like to acknowledge every woman who has motivated and inspired me to reach the place where I am today. I am very grateful for every word of encouragement, for every touch you placed on my shoulder, for every cheer and every laugh. We must keep the story going.

BIO

Bianca Zenkel grew up in a small town with limited career options lined up for her future. Pure grit and determination, and her focus on the next generation, led her to forge a new path for herself. Bianca has used her determination to go from airline hostess to the head of global events for a worldwide corporation. She has more than fourteen years of experience in marketing and corporate communication. She recently completed an MBA with a dissertation on women's leadership and is passionate about confidence and self-leadership—the two things that helped her conquer her mountaintop.

Notes

....

....

....

....

....

....

....

....

....

....

....

....

....

....

Milton Keynes UK
Ingram Content Group UK Ltd.
UKHW010706211123
432955UK00002B/5